The Stubbs

A comedy

Steve Harper

Samuel French—London
www.samuelfrench-london.co.uk

FOR AMATEUR PRODUCTION ENQUIRIES

UNITED KINGDOM AND WORLD
EXCLUDING NORTH AMERICA
plays@samuelfrench.co.uk
020 7255 4302/01

Each title is subject to availability from Samuel French, depending upon country of performance.

THE STUBBS

First performed at The Princess Theatre, Hunstanton, on 13th July 2012 with the following cast of characters:

Bill	Victor Tucker
Ethel	Anne Hyder
Violet	Evangelina Page
Trevor	Robert Hornet
Mrs Miller	Kathy Philipot
Toby Miller	Jack Hurst

Directed by Steve Harper
Designed by Steve Harper

CHARACTERS

Bill
Ethel
Violet
Trevor
Mrs Miller
Toby Miller

The action takes place in the sitting-room of the lodge of
Blennington Hall

Scene 1 An afternoon in May
Scene 2 Twenty-four hours later

Time—the present

Also by Steve Harper published by Samuel French

Lions and Donkeys

THE STUBBS
A play about being careful of what you wish for

The Browns' sitting-room. An afternoon in May

We are in the Browns' sitting-room which is in the lodge cottage of Blennington Hall. There is an external door L, *and the door to the kitchen* R. *On the back wall is a chimney breast and fireplace. The furniture has seen better days, and comprises a settee, a coffee table plus other assorted small pieces. The room is decorated with three or four cheap prints of framed "garish" art. A Tretchikoff (The Chinese Lady in Yellow Jacket) is over the mantelpiece, there is also a wall mirror near the door to the kitchen. Oh yes, and hidden away to the right of the chimney breast is a small George Stubbs oil painting of a racehorse in a gilt frame, circa 1798*

William Brown sits in the settee with one shoe off contemplating a large hole in the toe of his sock and holding a tube of bunion cream

Ethel Brown, his wife, enters laden with plates and tea cups for afternoon tea that she arranges on the coffee table after removing Bill's shoe

Bill Just look at this, I only had these at Christmas. Five months wear and they need darning.

Ethel (*arranging plates*) I think you'll find that darning went out with powdered egg and doodle bugs, dearest. I believe what today's gentleman about town does, is visit Marks and Spencer's fine emporium where he purchases a new pair.

Bill A new pair, but these only need a bit of mending, oh come on, Ethel, you'll weave your bit of magic with your sewing box and fix 'em, won't you? My mother used to …

Ethel Your mother, William, sainted woman though she was, could not perform miracles. (*Examining the sock distastefully*) What you would need to weave to resurrect these is not magic but Axminster. Throw them out. (*She looks at her watch*) But not right away. Right now, put your shoe on and get rid of the ointment. Violet is due back any time now with her new young man.

Bill (*putting the ointment away*) Spend, spend, spend, that's your answer to everything. You know what my old dad used to say: "Look after the pennies, and the pounds look after themselves". We need a back-up fund for our old age.

Ethel How many times have I heard this one? Look, we are not that short. Why don't we lash out, a holiday, a car … new socks. Come on, William, how much is in your little bank book now ?

Bill Ah, wouldn't you like to know. A damn site more than if we squandered it on new cars, holidays and new teeth for you.

Ethel (*examining her teeth in the mirror*) What do you mean new teeth, what's wrong with my teeth. You never mentioned my teeth before. They're good teeth they are.

Bill All I'm saying is, that if we want to retire to the seaside, like we talked about, we need a back-up fund. Do you know what you get for an old age pension now?

Ethel I haven't time to argue with you now. Violet will be here any minute.

Bill puts his shoe on

Ethel retreats to her kitchen, only to re-appear with a plate of sandwiches

Bill Oh sandwiches, are there any egg? I like egg.

Ethel There are some egg mayonnaise with black pepper and a dash of paprika.

Bill Ughhh. Ham then, any ham? You got some of that crumbed ham from Arkwright's, I saw the packet. He does do a nice bit of ham old Arkwright, even if his sausages are rubbish.
Ethel Yes, them, the brown ones near the middle.

Bill goes to take one, but has his hand slapped

Don't even think about it. These are for Violet's young man.
Bill What's he called again ?
Ethel He's called Trevor, Trevor Watson. You know sometimes I wonder if you listen to a word we say. We've been over this again and again.
Bill Oh yes, well let's see. He works in the big auction house near the river, er … Anchor's.
Ethel And …
Bill And it's his birthday, so Violet's bringing him here before they go out.
Ethel And ...
Bill And, er, Violet met him at her evening class. And his family is very hoity-toity and he went to some public school.
Ethel Winchester.
Bill Yeah, Winchester. He'll feel right at home here I shouldn't wonder. Sorry what I said about your teeth.

Ethel immediately turns to re-examine her teeth in the mirror, where-upon Bill pops a ham sandwich into his mouth

Ethel Oi! I saw that.

Doorbell

Bill They're here, blimey talk about saved by the bell.

Violet and Trevor enter R

Violet No need to ring the bell, silly. Mum, Dad, this is Trevor. Trevor this is my mum and dad.

Trevor Oh good afternoon, Mr Brown. (*He shakes hands*) Violet has told me so much about you. She didn't mention that you had a much younger wife though.

Ethel (*tittering*) Oh really now, Trevor, I'm not that much younger. And you must call us Ethel and William … or Bill.

Bill There's only eight months between us ...

Ethel Oh Bill, now stop, do. I hope you're feeling hungry, Trevor, we thought we would have afternoon tea today.

Trevor Starving

Violet I thought we were having tea on the lawn ?

Bill No, it's going to rain.

Trevor Oh do you think so, er … Bill.

Bill Yes, I do. I've got this bunion see, never fails, been giving me gyp all day. I was only just putting some cream on before you arrived.

Trevor Oh, (*looking at the hand he shook with Bill*) jolly good.

Ethel It will be nice to have it in here though, in the lounge.

Violet Yes of course, Mum, It was just that I was telling Trevor about the view of the hall from our back garden.

Trevor That's right, Blennington Hall, amazing old house, dates back to the sixteenth century apparently.

Bill Some of it does, a lot's been knocked down, and re-built. Cromwell took out the old tower with a bloody great cannon. Hitler managed to have a go at the west wing. The storm of '87 brought an oak down on the conservatory, and death watch beetle is doing its damndest to bring down parts of the old roof.

Violet Dad's quite an authority on Blennington.

Ethel And can talk for hours about it.

Trevor Have you lived here very long then, Bill?

Bill My dad was the handyman up there from 1943 right up to 1988.

Trevor Oh a handyman. So he came back during the war?

Bill Yes, he came back minus an arm, never thought he would get work, but old Lord Blennington had served in the same regiment and wasn't going to see Dad unemployed. I lived here all my life until I got married in '75. After Mum and Dad died the new Lord Blennington let Ethel and me have the cottage.

Ethel I come from Harrington, so when Bill and I were married we'd come over and see his parents. I know the hall quite well because Bill used to help his dad out when there was a two man job to be done.

Trevor You didn't take over from him then, Bill?

Violet Oh no, Dad had his own business by then.

Trevor So what do you do, Bill ?

Bill I'm a painter.

Trevor A painter, now that is interesting, where's your studio?

Pause

Oh you mean ...

Ethel He's the best painter and decorator in the county. He's done gold leaf and all-sorts.

Trevor Ah, emulsion rather then oils then.

Bill I do gloss work as well you know.

Ethel What about you, Trevor, what do you do?

Trevor Well, after Oxford Father managed to get me a post with Anchor's, he knows one of the partners. They're one of the better auction houses, do a lot of sub-contracting work for Sotheby's as a matter of fact. I'm in the fine art section, we do evaluations and category work, as well as sales. We deal with art worth millions.

Bill Blimey.

Ethel And you two are doing the same evening class?

Trevor Yes, Italian.

Violet We're doing conversations; *Nei Restorante* this week, Dad.

Bill Very nice. Go on then, say something in Eye-tie.

Trevor Oh, let's see. *Tesoro Viola, quanto tempo dobisiamo rimanere con loro?* [Violet darling, how long do we have to stay with them?]

Violet *Pazienza, sono andato a molta difficolta per il vostro compleanno.* [Patience, they have gone to a lot of trouble.]

Bill That's good What did you say?

Ethel Trevor asked how long he has to stay, and Violet told him to be patient.

Trevor (*aghast*) Oh, you speak Italian, Ethel.

Ethel Yes, done it at school for O level.

Trevor I feel rather silly now, but we are trying to practise whenever we can.

Ethel Yes, well I suppose it's all very handy for holidays and your work of course, Trevor. Lot of them painters was Italian weren't they? Some of them was very good, but my favourite is Mr Tretchikoff. He painted that one we've got over the fire-place. If you look, her eyes seem to follow you round the room.

Trevor Ah yes, The "Chinese Girl in Yellow Jacket", I believe.

Ethel Yes that's right. Oh Bill, Trevor knows about our picture.

Bill I don't know a lot about art, but I do know what I like. They wouldn't have it up at the hall. But then I wouldn't want half them old gloomy things they got up there.

Trevor I'd love to have a look at their collection, I don't suppose ——

Ethel (*quickly*) Right, let's get this tea organized, come on Violet, give me a hand.

Violet All right, Mum.

Violet and Ethel exit through to the kitchen

Bill So birthday boy today then, Trevor?

Trevor That's right. *Tempus fugit* as they say.

Pause

Look, Bill, I know you probably think I'm a bit of a "hooray", but Vi and I just, well really sort of hit it off from day one. That's not long, but for me she's a bit special, and I'd like to think I can offer her a bit more out of life.

Bill Oh yes, and what would that be then?

Trevor Well, the finer things, Bill, travel, money, a chance to move with the right set.

Bill And she wants these things, does she?

Trevor Oh Lord yes, I mean who wouldn't.

Bill So you have discussed this with her then?

Trevor No not yet, we've only just got to know each other. But I just thought it's better that we clear the air, you and I. I mean you're old school, Bill, different values. Whereas Violet and I are up for it. We want it all, and we want it now as the song goes.

Bill Yes, I think we understand each other now, Trevor. Thank you for that.

Trevor I knew you'd see it my way. Look, Bill, my father gave me this rather grand hip flask; and there's a drop of pretty good brandy in it, I don't suppose I could tempt you with a little?

Bill It's a bit early, but go on then, why not. It would be rather rude to refuse a drink on your birthday.

Trevor Any glasses?

Bill (*getting two tumblers from the mantelpiece*) These any good? (*He gets a grubby handkerchief from his pocket and gives them a good wipe*)

Trevor Good enough for five-star brandy, Bill ... (*He pours two generous measures*) Bottoms up!

Bill Cheers. (*He sits down*) Blimey that is a good drop of stuff.

Trevor I think we could go another, don't you?

Bill Most kind ...

They drink again

Trevor Might as well finish it off, Bill, here allow me. (*He pours a third measure for them both*) So, tell me, Bill, the Blenningtons have looked after your family over the years?

Bill (*slightly the worse for the brandy*) That's right, but it worked both ways. The old man made sure Dad had work when he was invalided out of the army and they got on pretty well all things considered. His son let Ethel and me stay on here after Dad's death, but we've had our uses.

Trevor How's that then?

Bill Well my old dad saved Lord Blennington's life you know.

Trevor No!

Bill He did, true as I'm sitting here. September 1944. Rescued him from a Junkers 88.

Trevor (*also feeling a little drunk*) No way ! Hang on, he wasn't even fighting in '44, and old Lord Blennington must have been over seventy.

Bill No, they wasn't on the front line, you tit. They was here, the Junkers was probably limping home after a raid, drops a single bomb, got lucky and hit the west wing of the hall.

Trevor Wow.

Bill Old Blennington goes scuttling down there, gets trapped in the burning cellar, and my dad rescued him, didn't he. Only had the one arm, but dragged his lordship clear of the fire, then bugger me he only goes back to drag out some of the treasures they sent up from London.

Trevor Treasures, Bill?

Bill (*after a pause*) Yeah. Well I shouldn't be talking about it really, but the war's been over a fair bit, don't suppose it's an official secret anymore.

Trevor This is intriguing stuff, Bill, you're sure you're not making this up?

Bill No. My old man told me the story himself. Old Lord Blennington was a mate of Churchill's. Served in South Africa together, didn't they. And Churchill knew the old man was a collector.

Trevor A collector?

Bill Paintings, real old ones.

Trevor So?

Bill So, Churchill's worried that the national art treasures will get destroyed in the blitz. So he sends them out to safe houses all over the country. Some went down Welsh mines, some went up to Scotland ... and some of them came here.

Trevor Wow.

Bill Anyway Churchill knew that the old man would know about storage conditions and the like. Can't have your Rembrandts getting soggy. So a big truck load of stuff from the National Gallery turns up here with an army escort, and my dad helps carry it down to the cellars under the west wing.

Trevor What were the paintings?

Bill I don't know, Dad said they was all crated up. Everything is signed for in triplicate, witnessed and signed for again. Foolproof really; well apart from a Junkers 88.

Trevor So it was all destroyed in the fire.

Bill Some was, but then the rest of the staff, and the local fire brigade, turned up and a lot was rescued. All the other crates got moved away. Don't know where they went, but old lord Bennington was pretty upset. Apparently he blamed himself. Least that's what he wanted people to think.

Trevor Go on.

Bill Any more of that brandy left?

Trevor Yes, I think there's enough for one more. Here you go. (*He pours the drink*)

Bill Ta. My old dad reckoned that not all the paintings that was reported as blown up, was blown up, if you get my drift.

Trevor Oh come on, Bill, this is getting to be a pretty tall tale. Listen, I'm in the art world, I think I would have heard about a massive art fraud like this if it were all true, don't you?

Bill You would have heard about it, son, if anybody believed it was true or if any of the paintings had gone back up for sale. But they never did. I told you, his lordship was a collector, he had enough money, didn't want to flog them. They might just as well have been blown up ...

Trevor No I'm sorry, Bill, I reckon you inherited your dad's ability to tell a good story, but that's all it is.

Ethel and Violet enter with tea, cakes and a gift-wrapped package

Ethel You was right, Bill, started to rain heavy now.

Violet You boys getting on all right?

Trevor Yes, we shared a drop of my birthday brandy, and Bill's been keeping me amused with some of his tall tales.

Bill I told you, Sonny-Jim, they ain't stories, it's what happened.

Ethel William Brown, where are your manners. You're always the same you are. You get a bit of drink in you, and you come over all argumentative. Now if Trevor's been kind enough to share his brandy with you I think the least you can do is say sorry. Well I never heard the like.

Trevor No, that's fine, Bill was just telling me about the bombing in 1944.

Ethel William, I think we'll say no more about the war, all right!

Bill Wasn't making it up. (*He gets up and walks to the fireplace*)

Violet Sorry, Trevor, Dad can get a bit maudlin at times. Anyway this is from all of us, happy birthday. (*She proffers the gift-wrapped package*)

Trevor Oh thank you. (*He opens the wrapping paper*) Oh, a tie, lovely.

Violet Yes, it's silk and it's got little anchors on it, so you can wear it to work …

Trevor Ah yes, as in Anchor's Auctioneers.

Ethel But see, we also had your initial put on to personalize it. We had it done on the internet, W for Watson.

Trevor Just so. Well not many of the chaps at work will have a tie with W Anchor on it, that's for sure.

Ethel Oh I'm pleased you like it. Right I'll be Mum. Tea, Trevor?

Trevor Yes please.

Violet Help yourself to sandwiches and cake.

They do so

Bill takes the small gilt-framed picture from the wall on the right side of the fireplace and shows it to Trevor

Bill Right, if it was all stories, how did my dad end up with this then?

Violet Mum.

Ethel William Brown, now you are just being plain rude. You are spoiling what was going to be a nice afternoon, waving

your dad's old horse picture around at Trevor like that. Now
sit down and be nice, and if you can't do that ——

Trevor takes the picture and stares at it, incredulous

Trevor Where did you get this from?
Bill I told you old Lord Blennington had a few of them destroyed
paintings snaffled away before you could say knife. Dad got
given this to keep him quiet after he helped shift them all. He
reckoned it reminded him of the 1940 Derby winner that he
won five bob on.
Trevor But this is a Stubbs.
Ethel No dear, it's definitely an 'orse.
Trevor I know this picture, I've seen prints of it, it was in the
National.
Bill That's right until it was destroyed in an air-raid in 1944.
Only like I keep telling you, it weren't.
Violet Trevor, you don't have to look at Dad's old painting, not
on your birthday.
Trevor No, you don't understand, any of you. This is a Stubbs, it
could be worth ... (*bit of quick thinking*) ... thousands of pounds.
Ethel No, what that old thing?
Trevor Yes, I'd have to verify its authenticity of course, but ——
Bill No, we don't want to sell it, I was just showing you it so
that you knew I wasn't making it all up.
Violet There, Dad doesn't want to sell, so we can get on with
our tea, then go out dancing like you said.
Ethel He might not want to sell it; but if it's worth that much ...
Trevor Exactly. The problem is of course provenance.
Ethel And what's that when it's at home?
Trevor Ownership.
Bill Well it's ours, been on that hook in the corner for, well must
be over sixty years.
Trevor Yes, but having it on your wall for that length of time
doesn't give you any right to sell it, Bill.
Bill Fair enough, I'll put it back.

Trevor No, there might be a way round that.
Ethel How's that then?
Violet   Nothing illegal, Trevor, these are my parents we're talking about.
Trevor Oh sure. Vi. But it's just that I know this, er, lady, who has bought the odd piece off of me in the past, without too many questions into their origins.
Bill But I don't want to sell, it was my dad's old painting.
Ethel Don't you stand there griping about the bloody price of socks when we've got an easier life staring us in the face. It must be ten years since you've taken that old thing down, look at the wallpaper behind it, I feel quite ashamed.
Trevor I would need to take it away to check it out.
Bill What do you mean?
Trevor Well it could be a forgery.
Violet So how would you know?
Trevor We have this machine at work called a chromatic spectrum analyzer.
Violet What does that do?
Trevor I burn a small amount of the sample.
Bill Now hold on, I'm not letting you burn my dad's painting.
Trevor Not the painting, Bill, just the dust and varnish flakes from inside the frame. That shows me the chemicals and trace elements present. I know what chemicals should be there for canvas, paint and varnish that's two hundred years old, and this will prove it within five years either way.
Ethel And how long would this take?
Trevor Well if I started right away, and do the necessary paper research as well, I could probably have an answer in twenty-four hours.
Violet Only we're going dancing ...
Trevor Sorry, old thing, but this is much more important.
Violet But you promised ...Well thank you very much.

Violet slams out R

Ethel Don't mind her, Trevor, you got plenty of nights to go dancing after you sorted all this.

Bill What's in it for you?

Trevor Well if, and it's a big if, this turns out to be a genuine Stubbs, the woman I've dealt with before pays me a finder's commission. So it wouldn't cost you anything.

Bill But if we ain't got a receipt?

Trevor I don't think Mrs Miller would be over troubled by that. She buys for a Russian collector, and he doesn't show his collection to anybody.

Ethel Go on then, go and get it sorted.

Bill reluctantly gives Trevor the painting

Trevor Look, I suppose I should just say that Mrs Miller, isn't the most, well, civilized of ladies. She and her son Toby have a bit of a reputation as tough nuts. Still, I expect she'll be pleased to meet you both! Just don't upset either of them, please.

Black-out

SCENE 2

The same. Twenty-four hours later

Bill is seated on the settee checking through his bank statements, using a calculator

Violet enters with cup of tea

Violet Here you are, Bill, That was Trevor on the phone, he's on his way over. Mrs Miller is with him, so it looks like good news.

Bill Well, he said twenty-four hours, (*looking at his watch*) and he wasn't far out. Right, you know what to do.

Violet Oh yes.

Ethel enters R

Ethel That's gone cold again. You can never trust May, I mean
yesterday, lovely day until the rain. Today, more like March
out there.
Bill Yes, we need to get away, and if this all goes OK perhaps
we'll go to the seaside.
Ethel Yes, I've been talking to Violet about that, and we've
come to an agreement ——

Doorbell

Violet Right, that's them. Everybody set?
Bill What's this agreement about then?
Ethel Not now, Bill, we'll discuss it later.

Ethel goes out to the front door

(*Off*) Oh hello, Trevor, do come in.

Trevor enters R *with Mrs Miller and her son Toby. Mrs Miller is
overdressed in an expensive but tasteless outfit. Toby is wearing
sunglasses and is dressed in a suit. He exudes menace. These
are not nice people! Trevor is carrying the picture, which is
wrapped, and seems a tad nervous. Ethel follows them in*

Trevor Good afternoon, Mr Brown, Mrs Brown, Violet. This is
Mrs Miller and her son Toby.
Mrs Miller (*sitting down uninvited*) Pleased to meet you all
I'm sure.
Toby (*standing behind his mother*) Yes, pleased to meet you.
Trevor We all know why we're here, so I'll come to the point.
Toby Good.
Trevor Mr and Mrs Brown have in their possession a work
of art.

*Trevor takes the wrapping off the Stubbs and places it on
mantelpiece, where they all contemplate it for a moment*

Bill That's my dad's horse picture that is.

Trevor Yes and I'm pleased to inform you all that after extensive tests I can now confirm this is a George Stubbs original. It was painted in 1798 and until now believed lost in an air raid in 1944. Consequently there are no papers relating to ownership.

Toby What tests ?

Trevor Ah yes, tests. Well as I explained to Mr and Mrs Brown I have access to a chromatic spectrum analyzer at work. I went in alone last night and used it. The results show conclusively that the age of the canvas, frame, varnish and paint are two hundred and twelve years old. The brush strokes, subject and signature confirm that they are without doubt the work of George Stubbs. The records show that this particular painting was hung in the National Gallery until 1944 when an air raid destroyed it, and that would concur with the information supplied by Mr Brown.

Toby So what your saying is, it's Kosher.

Trevor Er, yes.

Mrs Miller Right dear, never mind all the clever technical stuff. I don't know a lot about that. What I know about is people. Now look into my eyes and tell me I'm not wasting my money.

Trevor I assure you, Mrs Miller —— (*He sits*)

Mrs Miller Before you give me your assurance, Trevor dear, you had better understand the ramifications of me being stitched up like a kipper. Toby, would you explain to Mr Watson.

Toby Yes, Mum.

Violet I think we all understand, Mrs Miller.

Mrs Miller Yes dear, I'm sure we do, but, when it comes to financial matters, I like everything to be crystal. Toby, would you do the honours.

Toby I will, Mum, excuse me a moment.

Toby exits L

Ethel So are you interested in our painting for yourself, Mrs Miller?

Mrs Miller No, dear. I'm what you call an entrepreneur . I buy, I sell, I make a small profit. There is a certain Russian gentleman of my acquaintance what collects things. Yachts, football clubs, islands…an oily-garck.   At present he has become focused on the art world. And I think he might be interested in your picture, even though you ain't got no proof of ownership. But let's just hear what Trevor has to say first.

Toby enters with a large pair of bolt cutters

Trevor Actually I don't have a lot to add, Mrs Miller.
Mrs Miller Toby.
Toby Right. Would you stand up a minute, Mr Watson.
Trevor (*rising*) Er, yes OK. Why exactly?

Toby punches Trevor very hard in the stomach

Toby It just makes this a bit easier.

Trevor sinks back into his chair winded. Toby then puts Trevor's left foot on the coffee table, and removes his shoe and sock

Ethel Here, there's no need for that.
Mrs Miller I have to disagree with you there, my dear. Unpleasant yes, but definitely necessary. (*She starts to make up her face with a compact as the mirror*)
Toby Now, you're not going to be able to talk for a moment. So just listen and I'll tell you about a little game we are going to play.
Trevor Aghhhhhhh.
Toby The game is called "This little piggy went to market". What happens is I ask a question, and if I think you're telling porkies — (*turning to his mum*) — did you hear that, Mum, porkies!
Mrs Miller Yes, Toby, very droll.
Toby Anyway, if I do, then I snips off a little piggy. Only we play it back to front and we start with the little pig that went wee, wee, wee all the way home. (*To Mr Brown*) I'll bet you don't know why we do that?

Mr Brown Now look, son ——

Toby We do it, because if we snips off the little pig that went to market first, then poor old Trevor here would never walk proper again. You need your big toe to walk. I read that in Mum's *Woman's Own*. Can you talk yet, Trev?

Trevor (*sucking in air*) Yes.

Toby Good. (*He fits the bolt cutters over Trevor's little toe*)

Violet Oh for God's sake, Mrs Miller, make him stop.

Mrs Miller I wouldn't make any unnecessary loud noises, dear, not now!

Toby Right, your starter for ten. Did you do all them tests that you said?

Trevor Yes, oh Jesus, yes. Please, Toby, don't.

Toby That's good, Trev, 'cos I believe you. Let's try another, shall we. Did all your tests show the painting was the genuine article?

Trevor Yes, yes, Toby, it was all good, please.

Toby Right. Did you tell anybody else about the painting, and, Trevor, I do mean anybody.

Trevor No, nobody, Toby, please, I didn't tell anybody.

Toby So far so good, and look, Trev, you still have ten little appendages. Right, next question. (*He pauses*) What is the capital of Venezuela?

Trevor (*nearly wetting himself*) What? Oh God, I don't know. Oh please, Toby, I don't know. Please don't, please …

Toby No, I was just joking, that wasn't the real question. I just thought I'd lighten the situation a little. Right final question. Now listen carefully. Do you ever want to play "This little piggy" again?

Trevor No, Toby, I don't, I don't ever want to again. Please, Toby, don't cut me. Please.

Toby Is the right answer. Right, now if you talk to anybody about this deal, Trevor — and once again I do mean anybody — I will find you and we will play again; but I won't be so nice! Do you believe me?

Trevor Yes, I mean no, I mean yes, I won't tell anybody, Trevor, I won't, I won't.

Mrs Miller Right that will do, Toby, put 'em away. (*She snaps shut the compact case*)
Toby Yes, Mum.
Mrs Miller He's a good boy for his old mum.
Bill Children can be such a blessing.
Mrs Miller That's right, dear, yes. Right, Trevor, I'm sorry you had to go through that, but you need to realize we ain't playing at this. Now here is a little finder's fee for you. (*She hands over a brown envelope from her handbag*) Now take your shoe and your sock and go.
Trevor Thank you, thank you.
Mrs Miller Oh and, Trevor.
Trevor Yes Mrs Miller?
Mrs Miller If ever you come across any other little; collectibles, you'll be sure and let me know first — won't you, dear?
Trevor Yes, Mrs Miller, I will, I swear I will.
Mrs Miller Good boy, off you go then.

Trevor exits crying, clutching his shoe, sock and envelope

Bill You're not going to try any rough stuff on us are you?
Mrs Miller Good heavens no, Mr Brown, now we have established your bona-fides this has become a business matter. Quite simply I will offer you a very large sum of cash, which obviously you will accept and we will leave with the painting. No receipts or paperwork will change hands. None of this ever happened if you get my drift! What could be simpler?
Violet Sounds all right, Dad.
Toby Now you sound like a nice sensible girl, Violet isn't it? Perhaps we could get to know each other after all this is settled.
Violet I don't like violence, Mr Miller, and I like you even less. All in all I think I'd rather go back to Trevor, even if he is a spineless coward. I tell you, Mr Toby Miller, if I were a man you wouldn't have frightened me like that.
Mrs Miller Leave it, Toby, we don't mix business and pleasure.
Toby Yes, Mum

Mrs Miller And,Violet dear, if you thought that was scary, you're being naïve.

Ethel (*going to the painting and looking at it* All right, let's get this over with. You want the painting, what's your offer?

Mrs Miller Well that's direct, and I like that. Right, my dear, now considering this is a one-off situation, you ain't never going to get a chance to sell this old painting again because it ain't yourn to sell. I am going to make what I think is a very generous offer.

Bill That sounds all right.

Violet How generous?

Mrs Miller I have here in my handbag, in cash, two hundred thousand pounds.

Stunned silence

Bill Blimey.

Violet Oh Dad.

Toby More then generous, Mum.

Ethel No!

More stunned silence

Bill What do you mean no? That's two hundred thou we just been offered.

Ethel I mean no, it ain't enough.

Violet Mum.

Mrs Miller Not enough, what do you mean not enough? It looks to me like you ain't got a pot to piss in, and your turning down nearly a quarter of a million.

Ethel I went to the library.

Toby And.

Ethel They got the internet down there you can use.

Bill What did you look up ?

Ethel Our painting, it's what Trevor said, they think it was blown up in 1944, but they had another one just like it and that sold at auction in Japan last year.

Violet How much, Mum?

Ethel Nine point four million pounds.

Bill Bloody hell!

Mrs Miller Yes, but what you got to remember is that was a legal deal. This ain't . That was sold to some museum what can put it on show. Not like this one, dear, not like this at all.

Violet But even so, nine point four million …

Toby Oh get real, darling, we're talking stolen goods here. Two hundred large is a good offer.

Bill Ethel!

Ethel No.

Mrs Miller All right, I didn't want it this way but; Toby get the painting for your old mum.

Toby Yes, Mum.

Toby turns and approaches Ethel. As he does so she produces a Stanley knife out of her pocket

Toby Oh come on, lady, you don't want to do that.

Bill Ethel, put it away.

Mrs Miller I really don't think Toby is going to let you cut him, Mrs Brown.

Ethel (*picking up the Stubbs*) Oh I'm not going to cut Toby, but I just might take a big slice out of this old painting.

Toby Mum?

Mrs Miller You don't want to do that, dear, that could spoil everything for all of us, tell her, Bill.

Bill I think she's very determined, Mrs Miller. I mean what have we got to lose, that old painting that none of us really noticed over the last sixty years. No, I think she's made her mind up.

Toby (*advancing*) Right!

Mrs Miller Wait a moment, Toby dear. I don't think even you could stop her cutting that canvas. Let's all calm down and have a little think.

Violet I think if you made a higher offer, Mrs Miller, it might resolve all our problems.

Mrs Miller Oh yes. Well, I don't like to see no-one unresolved. If I was to dip into Toby's share of the profits I could go, well let's say a quarter mill?
Toby Mum!
Bill Ethel?
Ethel It's still a long way off nine point four million, isn't it?

Pause

Mrs Miller Four hundred thousand pounds, and that's the last offer that Toby will leave here with a smile on his little face. And believe me, Mrs Brown, you do not want him to leave here unhappy.
Violet Now, I don't know of course, but I would think you have already set up a deal with your Russian friend, giving you a very healthy profit. And I would also think that a man that rich would employ even bigger and nastier minders then Toby here, and that they might be paying you a visit with their tool bags if the painting doesn't arrive in one bit as promised.

Pause

Mrs Miller How would you feel about a cheque?
Bill No cheques.
Mrs Miller All right, what we seem to have here then is a Mexican stand-off. So I'm going to tell you what's going to happen.
Violet Go on.
Mrs Miller I have in my bag, a plan B.
Bill And what's that when it's at home?
Mrs Miller Plan B, Bill, is a banker's draft, do you know what that is?
Ethel I do, that bloke paid for our car with one two years ago.
Mrs Miller Yes, you could do that, because what it is, it's a cheque, but it's drawn on a bank, not on an account. You can present it at any bank anywhere in the world, and they will cash it for you. Understand?
Bill So it's a good as cash then?

Mrs Miller Better, Bill, because you won't give yourself a hernia lifting it.
Ethel How much is it for?
Mrs Miller Ah, now there's the problem, you see this is already made out to you, and the amount is already written in. I can't change it. This was my fall back, my last offer in case anything went wrong.
Bill Which it has.
Mrs Miller Yes, which it has. So last offer. (*Pause*) Five hundred thousand. Deal or no deal?
Bill Come on, Ethel love.
Violet Mum, that's a lot of money.

All look at Ethel

Ethel (*positioning the Stanley knife in the middle of the canvas*) The banker's draft and two-fifty, or I turn "Dobbin" here into a pantomime horse, and we get half each.
Toby Three quarters of a mill, your having a laugh.
Violet Think about it, Toby, you're getting it for less then ten per cent of its true value. I'm sure you and you're mum are smart enough not to be out of pocket at that price, and this way nobody gets hurt. Right?
Toby Mum?
Mrs Miller I'm thinking. (*Pause*) All right seven hundred and fifty. But if this goes tit's up Toby will be back, clear?
Ethel (*putting down the knife*) All right.

Mrs Miller hands over the banker's draft plus cash, Toby collects the painting

Mrs Miller I won't say it's been a pleasure doing business with you, but I think we both came out ahead. I hope I don't need to remind you that none of this happened, and we never met. Are we agreed?
Bill Believe me, Mrs Miller, you will never hear from any of us ever again.

Mrs Miller Good, I'll bid you good afternoon then.

Toby and Mrs Miller exit, Toby carrying the bolt cutters and painting

Toby (*leaving*) Last chance to change your mind, darling. No? Ah well.

All three gather round to look at their money

Ethel I feel a bit queer, Bill.
Bill I'll put the kettle on.

Bill exits R

Violet Now, when he comes back, we're agreed aren't we?
Ethel Yes, I'm getting too old for this.

Bill enters R *with another wrapped painting under his arm*

Bill Just waiting for the kettle.
Ethel Oh Bill, seven hundred and fifty thousand, whatever next?

Long pause. Bill removes the wrapping

Bill Well, next I thought we'd have a go with this Lowry, *Street Scene*, 1947. (*He reveals the painting*)
Violet Oh I quite like that, is it finished?
Bill Yes, authentic dust, dirt and varnish from Salford circa 1947, and more importantly it's painted on board, not canvas, mean bugger Lowry.
Ethel You are a clever old thing, how long did it take you to paint that one?
Bill Not as long as the Stubbs, but they're completely different techniques of course.
Ethel Right, Bill, we all have something to talk about.

Bill (*looking a little worried*) You're not having a baby, Ethel, are you?

Ethel Sauce. Now look, Bill, how much have we got in the retirement fund now?

Bill Well, difficult to put an exact number to it, what with variable interest rates, and exchange rates ...

Ethel So give us a round about figure then.

Bill (*consulting his savings book*) With today's little addition ...

Ethel Yes.

Bill And using yesterdays closing Footsie index ...

Ethel Bill!

Bill Well, roughly twenty-eight point five-three million pounds.

Violet We have been busy, haven't we.

Ethel Right. Bill, that's enough. We work well as a team, but let's not push our luck. Violet and I agree it's time to pack it in and enjoy life. She is off to Italy.

Violet I've found a nice little house on the shore of Lake Garda.

Violet exits R, *to reappear with three small suitcases*

Ethel And I've found a nice little place by the seaside.

Bill Frinton?

Ethel No, Bill, not Frinton. Union Island, it's seventy miles north west of St Lucia, in the Caribbean. You can paint Gauguins on the veranda.

Bill Oh, and you're both sure that's what you want?

Violet Sure, Bill.

Ethel Yes, me too, Bill.

Bill Two on to one then. What are the travel arrangements, Ethel?

Ethel (*producing three passports and a pile of documents from her handbag*) We are Mr Henry and Mrs Verity McLouth, retired on a good income after a life in the Aberdeen grocery business.

Bill Verity?

Ethel Well, I like Verity. Violet, you are Mrs Jennifer Jones, recently widowed from your wealthy car-dealer husband.

Violet Jennifer Jones, yes I like that. At least they're an improvement on William, Ethel and Violet. Where on earth did you dream them up, Henry ?
Bill Did you never read Richmal Crompton, my dear. The "Just William" stories. Ethel was his sister, and Violet was ——
Violet Oh yes now I remember, Violet Elizabeth Bott.

Violet and Bill chant together the punchline associated with Violet Elizabeth Bott

Ethel Right. Jennifer, here's a cheque for, let's see, twenty-eight point five-three divided by three. (*She writes a cheque*)
Violet I'll call it nine and a half if Bill, sorry Henry, will throw in that Lowry, I can see that on the wall of my villa.
Bill Done. Right, I presume we have trains to catch. Is the rent on this place all paid up, er, Verity?
Ethel Yes, all loose ends tidied up. (*Handing over the cheque*) Right, we should go. Do you think Trevor will be all right?
Bill Oh yes, he was necessary to plant the idea, but the real trick as always is greed. They all wanted to believe, and that's why they did. .My old dad used to say ——
Ethel Yes, Henry, I know. "Be careful of what you wish for; you just might get it."

All three exit L with cases and Violet is also carrying the painting

BLACK-OUT

FURNITURE AND PROPERTY LIST

Scene 1

On stage: Settee
Coffee table. *On it*: tube of bunion cream, **Bill**'s sock with large hole in toe, **Bill**'s shoe
Fireplace. *On mantelpiece*: two tumblers. *Above mantelpiece*: Tretchikoff's *The Chinese Lady in Yellow Jacket. To* R: small George Stubbs oil painting of a racehorse c. 1798 in a gilt frame
3 or 4 cheap prints of "garish" art
Wall mirror near kitchen door
2 tumblers

Off stage: Tray with teacups and saucers, plates (**Ethel**)
Plate of sandwiches (**Ethel**)
Pot of tea, plate of cakes (**Ethel**)
Gift-wrapped tie (**Violet**)

Personal: **Ethel**: wristwatch
Bill: wristwatch, grubby handkerchief in pocket
Trevor: hip flask containing brandy

Scene 2

Strike: Tube of bunion cream
Tray, teapot, teacups and saucers, plates, cakes, sandwiches, Stubbs painting

Set: Bank statements and calculator for **Bill**
Ethel's handbag containing 3 passports, cheque book and pen, pile of documents

Off stage: Cup of tea (**Violet**)
                 Stubbs painting wrapped in paper (**Trevor**)
                 Large pair of bolt cutters (**Toby**)
                 3 small suitcases (**Violet**)

Personal: **Mrs Miller**: handbag containing compact with mirror,
                     brown envelope with money, banker's draft
                 Ethel: Stanley knife in pocket
                 Bill: savings' book

LIGHTING PLOT

Property fittings required: nil

Interior. The same scene throughout

To open: General interior lighting

Cue 1   **Trevor**: "Just don't upset either of them, please."   (Page 13)
            Black-out

Cue 2   To open Scene 2   (Page 13)
            Bring up general interior lighting

Cue 3   **Verity**: "' ... you just might get it.'" They exit   (Page 25)
            Black-out

EFFECTS PLOT

Cue 1   **Ethel**: "Oi! I saw that."   (Page 3)
Doorbell

Cue 2   **Ethel**: "... and we've come to an agreement —— " (Page 14)
Doorbell